Heal the World with Kindness

-Sibel Terhaar-

About the Author

Sibel Terhaar is a kindness activist and international author. Her inspirational messages on social media have motivated and captured millions of hearts looking for kindness in a challenging world.

Sibel was born the youngest of two children in Ankara, Turkey. Her parents were brought up in Eastern Turkey and were married at the young age of fourteen. Sibel had many hardships as a child. Her father suffered from many addictions and was abusive, and as a result, they lived in poverty and often went without food for days. Sibel questioned how the world could be such a cruel place; because of this, the slightest act of kindness was life-changing and felt like finding a drop of water in a barren desert.

During her teen years, Sibel was not allowed to participate in activities outside school except visiting her local library. She spent hours reading Shakespeare, King David, and many others. Every page she read was an adventure and an escape from her experiences at home, but one book changed Sibel's life: How to Win Friends & Influence People by Dale Carnegie.

Dale spoke about smiling, showing a genuine interest in people, and God's love. It was then that Sibel decided to incorporate these principles into her life. She made it her mission to engage with everyone she could and positively influence others. In college, Sibel had an opportunity to share her perspective with others as a host of a popular radio station. It was one of the best experiences in her life, and it was then that she felt she had finally found her voice.

Sibel immigrated to the United States in 2003 and started a new life with her husband as they raised a family. In 2020, during the COVID-19 pandemic, Sibel had another opportunity to share messages of hope and kindness, this time on LinkedIn. She started posting quotes about kindness and life on LinkedIn, and the response was overwhelming. Her messages resonated with many, and she continued networking and building a community of like-minded people striving for a kinder world.

Today, Sibel continues to post messages of hope and kindness on LinkedIn and other social media platforms.

Thank you for reading *Heal the World with Kindness.*

I hope this book will inspire and motivate you to keep kindness, hope, and love as the foundation of all you endeavor to do in life.

This book is dedicated to the loving memory of Judy.

This world is broken, and the struggle is great.

Despite our differences, we must unite and heal the world with kindness.

Although the world may push against you and entice you to shelter in its storm, never relent and continue chasing kindness against the wind.

Today is the day for your breakthrough; you only need to believe.

Start by expecting the best for yourself and giving your best to others.

You can start over at 20.

You can start over at 30.

You can start over at 40.

You can start over at 50.

You can start over at 60.

You can start over at 70.

Don't ever feel it's too late to do what you love and begin again!

The right opportunity will knock on your door one day, and on that day, the script will flip, and your future will be rewritten.

Don't ever stop challenging yourself, even in failure.

Progress is the result when discipline meets passion.

Choosing to smile is a decision to create your destiny.

Sharing it with others is a commitment to change the world.

Your gentle heart deserves true love.

Never give it away to someone who would break it into pieces.

The mind is an incredible but also a devious masterpiece.

It will tell you the most wonderful lies and lead you to believe dangerous things about yourself.

It is good to hold a mirror up to your conscience daily and make sure you recognize who you see on the other side.

Loving yourself is a victory but loving others is the reward.

I've often thought about what could have been and what I would change if I had the chance to begin again.

Despite my regrets, I would choose this life a thousand times and find myself happy with today.

A sacred love dwells inside a strong woman, and anything less given in return will never be enough for her.

Truth does not need
permission to speak.

Trying to silence the
truth is like hiding the
sun's warmth with
your hand.

Your next breakthrough is on the other side of rejection.

Never give up, and trust that success is around the corner.

There is a beautiful world out there.

When was the last time you raised your hands to greet the sun on a warm day?

When was the last time you breathed the crisp night air and counted the stars?

When was the last time you smiled at a stranger and said hello?

It's a beautiful world out there, and it's waiting for you.

Whether you are appreciated or not, you must give your best in all situations.

At the end of the day, you must be content with yourself and trust that you will reap what you sow.

When success knocks at your door, it may come as an unfamiliar face and look different than what you expected.

It is neither a friend nor enemy but, instead, a traveler that has no loyalty and cares not to linger.

You are a prisoner to no one or place or moment in time.

The decision to change your life is yours and yours alone.

Be courageous
enough to love
without restraint.

Selfishness is a dense
fog that only serves
to blind us from the
world.

If you find it hard to forgive yourself, start with forgiving someone else.

Whatever is worth fighting for, fight for it now.

When your conscience objects, speak up before it's too late.

Truth demands to be heard, and waiting will only delay justice.

Never waste a night with anxious thoughts that trouble your mind.

Instead, let yourself dream of tomorrow and all that is possible while you can.

Be selective with whom you listen to and follow.

Their messages are investments for the soul, and the payout should always be to your benefit.

My dreams are not always achieved, and my hopes are sometimes abandoned.

Yet I know that one day all the pieces will come together, and all will be as it should.

Pursue your happiness and strive to be the reason for others' happiness.

The seeds of kindness you plant today may one day return to be harvested and will nourish your soul.

Jealousy is a threat to the soul.

Peace cannot exist alongside jealousy; joy abounds with charity and love.

It can be hard to overcome, but happiness is the result, and love is the reward.

When you make an important decision, don't rush through the journey.

Good things take time.

It may be difficult and bring pain, but everything works together as it should.

If you want to reach your goal, pursue it by focusing on the skills to get you there.

Without direction, you'll only find yourself going through the motions.

Pursue your passion, set a goal, and work hard to achieve your dream.

We all have difficulties in our lives, but we also have the power to overcome them.

If you care about yourself, find a way out of your situation.

One of the best ways to feel love and hope is by providing it to others.

Find someone in your life, give them hope, and love them unconditionally.

You are beautiful, smart, and extraordinary.

Your smile is a melody that will be sung for ages.

Your heart is arrayed in gold and kindness for all to see.

You are ready for your journey, and you will prevail.

Some of the most beautiful smiles are buried under broken hearts.

Sometimes people will not understand your kindness.

They may reject and mock you, but never let it discourage you.

You are kind because your heart demands it.

You have nothing to prove but everything to give.

Life is a team sport.

You must surround yourself with positive and like-minded people to stay strong in a challenging world.

Sometimes our wounds are
so deep that we cannot feel
God through the pain.

We may feel abandoned but
trust that He is not absent in
his silence.

His promise endures, and
He will mend our wounds
and make us whole again.

Roar with all you have against the voices of doubt.

Let your confidence shine upon the providence that is laid out before you.

Every great story includes a comeback.

Life may have you on the ropes today, but tomorrow is yours to write.

We should not forget that we are all human and fall from time to time.

It is easy to fall and hard to get back up, but that is where resilience is forged, and growth occurs.

Share your smile and let it sail across oceans.

The winds of promises will deliver it to people in need.

Those who have kind hearts can make miracles happen.

They open the doors of heaven and allow its light to shine on the world.

Never forget how far you've come.

Celebrate your growth.

The purpose of life is not found in success, wealth, or a career.

The purpose of life is found in the relationships we have, the moments we create, and the love we share.

No matter how much
this world tries to
bend your will, do
not relent.

Stay strong and be
courageous.

Never give up on the
dreams that inspire
you to live.

You'll never grow
in life if you get
upset about being
wrong.

Be wise and lower
the shield of pride
that's battling the
enemy within.

Your soul remains forever young, and love is possible at any age.

When your heart is broken, remember that Juliet wasn't Romeo's first love, and you can love again.

Never apologize for being you and for the way you feel.

Hurt the way you hurt, live the way you live, and love the way you love.

Climbing the highest mountain is a lot like being kind.

It can be a challenge, but the view from the top is breathtaking.

Each day is a new
opportunity to
create a vision and
plan for success.

The first step is
believing it's
possible.

Self-love is not putting yourself first and others last; it is denying your ego and serving others.

Live your life like a legend, with honor and grace.

Never compromise your character for fame or wealth.

Pursuing these things are meaningless, like chasing after the wind.

There are billions of us, but only a few will dare to change the world.

Although tomorrow is a new day, its fabric is woven from the threads you bind today.

Nothing can stand in the way of your achievements except your own doubt.

The crown of your success comes from your character, not your position.

The pain you have within is no match for the power of your smile.

The morning is a declaration for those who endeavor to achieve with virtuous intent.

You will find a way to forget and learn how to love again.

When you walk with God, no one can change your direction.

Her spirit endures, and her lessons stay with us forever.

No matter how much we are loved, no one will love us like our mother.

The biggest flex is remaining calm in the face of an insult.

No matter how hard it tries, the world cannot ignore your kindness.

Keep your anger private and your kindness known.

Sometimes it's best to wait and listen.

The world is not going anywhere.

The most beautiful time is now, and the possibilities are endless.

In all your travels, always bring your kindness first and your belongings second.

Great things are inevitable when you see life as a promise of endless opportunities.

The word sorry is powerful, much like love.

Never say either without sincerity.

If you are having a bad day, turn it around!

Change the room you are sitting in, grab your favorite drink, watch something funny, or throw yourself into nature.

Don't be content with negativity; empower yourself by choosing your mood.

A minute spent in reflection may change your life forever.

Never forget to appreciate the people who gave you a chance.

The power of money is temporary, but the power of kindness is eternal.

I would not choose people, careers, or money over my faith in God, but without His help, I would choose wrong every time.

You will break your heart when you allow others to trample what you should be protecting.

An unexpected act of kindness is the best.

Surprise them!

Controlling your emotions can make you unpredictable and powerful.

Train yourself, and you will grow.

Be careful not to tell everyone everything.

Privacy protects you and your next move.

Stop obsessing over your mistakes.

Accept your failures, forgive yourself, and learn to move on.

Be open to criticism without offense.

That's when the real conversation starts.

Silence is a strength when everyone is loud.

Love is the first move of a warrior who battles for peace.

The secret to leading others is appreciating them.

Healing begins with making your well-being the priority and ends with helping others.

No one can fulfill the purpose of your life except you.

We were not
created to rush
through this life.

Slow down and
enjoy all you have in
front of you before
it's over.

Don't despair.

There is an unknown warrior within you that is ready to fight your battle today.

It's not about their acceptance or rejection; it's about the reasons you fight and the purpose within you.

Love is a magical story that is written by the heart.

Don't focus on the possibility of rejection; instead, focus on your inevitable success.

You did nothing wrong, removing the toxic people from your life and prioritizing yourself.

Your gentle heart had enough.

You cannot treat others with contempt but seek God's grace for yourself.

Asking for a blessing while being a curse to others is no way to live.

Never let anyone catch you with your head down.

Keep your head up!

Be proud of yourself regardless of what you are going through in life.

You may think knowing oneself would be easy but knowing what you're capable of and then acting on that knowledge is one of life's greatest challenges.

A broken heart can heal with time, but first comes clarity and possibly regret.

Don't let the window of tomorrow fog over because a new day will come, and the sun will rise again.

One beautiful word can mend two broken hearts.

Defeat is a wicked sting that is not soon forgotten.

We forge ahead with the lessons learned and become stronger to fight another day.

We will be ready when the stakes are at their highest, and the taste of victory will never leave our lips.

You are important, a
there is a reason you we.
created.

The world needs you
more than you could ever
imagine.

Your purpose can bring
love, peace, and kindness
to many, but only if you
allow it.

When problems seem exhausting, remember this promise.

You will endure and never be given more than you can handle.

Never give up hope and trust that all things work for the greater good.

Being humble lifts you and will never let you down.

When you are humble, you will understand people better.

When you understand people, it is easier to accept them.

When you accept them for who they are, you will never be disappointed.

When you are not disappointed in others, you will be happier in this life.

Humility takes you on the path you've longed for, the path of inner peace.

Distance yourself from those who do not value a kind heart.

You need courageous friends who value your heart and will not exploit your vulnerabilities.

One day a true friend will come into your life.

They will walk with you, side by side, and you will find comfort in their company.

Never let them go, and hold them close with all that you have within you.

Striving for perfection in life is a miserable way to live.

Enjoy the journey, learn from your mistakes, and forgive yourself along the way.

I believe we have good in all of us, but it's up to each of us how much we choose to use it.

Be kind to those who have treated you unfairly.

I know it is hard, but it paves the way to a better world you help create.

It is never too late to turn around.

Choose today to start a new journey.

Some people will not understand that you are trying to heal.

They are quick to judge without knowing your past and the future you are trying to build.

Forgive them and hope for their healing as well.

When dealing with an unfair situation, speak honestly and leave your fear behind.

In the end, trust in God, no matter the outcome.

My heart aches for those hurting, but my respect is undying for those who choose to forgive and overcome their hardships with kindness and love.

Surround yourself with the people who push you to level up, catch you when you fall, and defend you at your worst.

The fog will lift, and the sun will shine once again.

Have hope for tomorrow and the promise of eternity.

Let love find a home in your heart, and never abandon it to fear.

When someone offends you, let kind words be your defense.

A great leader will
fill a room with
energy and
encourage creativity.

A poor leader will
discourage ideas with
ignorance.

Maturity is focusing on the greater good rather than yourself.

Self-care isn't just for the weekends.

You deserve attention every day.

Turning the cheek is not a message of weakness.

It is about standing your ground in faith and trusting God's justice.

Even if people don't deserve you, be kind and show them love.

Be a healer!

Don't wait for better days; they're already here waiting for you to make the most of them.

Life doesn't start tomorrow; never forget that.

Leaving a toxic relationship is an act of bravery, not an act of defeat.

Your kindness and hard work shall not be in vain.

Whether it is luck or coincidence, the mystery of why we have met is unknown, yet meaningful.

Joy is found where time and distractions are not welcome.

The wisest mind takes the boldest action.

Starting your day with a positive mindset is the new breakfast of champions.

It is our nature to bond and comfort each other when faced with hardship and tragedy.

Imagine what the world could be if we united through our aspirations and not our collective sorrow.

It's time to stop encouraging overworking and sleepless nights.

Burning the candle at both ends will only leave you in the dark.

When dealing with ugly things, don't be discouraged and saddened.

This shall pass; remember, there is a promised inheritance beyond this world that is pure and unblemished.

Don't be surprised when bad things in life begin to fade and good things come your way.

Be happy because God is working in your life.

Most of us carry a beautiful heart but are afraid to share it with the world.

No matter how big your dreams may seem, the right mindset and discipline can make the impossible happen!

We must seek
happiness in our
lives at the
intersection of
love, forgiveness,
and truth.

Everyone will have to face the truth eventually.

Some will live embracing it, others will run from it, but no one will escape it.

If someone doesn't respond to your kindness, give them space, and leave them in peace.

It may take time to chip away at someone's anger, and you may be the first to have tried, but hopefully, you are not the last.

Sometimes you must make tough decisions and stand up for justice; some may mock and slander you for your decision.

It doesn't make you difficult; it means you have the character to stand up for the truth.

Don't expect to succeed every day.

You will have different levels of energy each day.

Some days you will feel extremely motivated, energetic, and driven.

Some days, you'll feel weak, bored, and uninspired.

The key is to keep going and never let the bad days stop you from progressing.

Whatever you value
in life, make kindness
the foundation.

Its strength will never
fail you.

The greatest defeat in life is letting hatred take over your soul.

The solution to unfair treatment is to speak up.

Being happy in the workplace has a ripple effect at home, with family, and throughout society.

It breaks my heart to see people struggle with mental health.

We may see a smile on the surface, but we have no idea what someone is going through deep down inside.

One day, kindness will rule the world.

The more I choose to serve others, the closer I get to the heart of God.

Rejection is only a delay on the road to victory.

True wisdom is gained from the clarity that comes from being broken.

Capability is not born from skills or experience.

It's merely a choice to say, "Yes, I can do this."

If you made a mistake, forgive yourself.

If you were rejected, try again.

Life is the ultimate teacher, and our experiences prepare us for tomorrow's opportunities.

I am sticking with being happy and grateful despite all the twists and turns in my life.

When feeling down
and overcome with
doubt, remind
yourself that you
deserve to be
treated well and are
worthy of love.

You are kind because you choose to be.

Chase your dreams relentlessly and never give up or let others dissuade you from all you aim to achieve.

No one else can do the things you dream of, and it's up to you to see them come true.

People who help you when you are at your lowest are the most important people!

Even when you fear that all is lost, God is a God of miracles.

Real influence is driven by character, not money or popularity.

The first step towards being brave often involves taking a step back.

When people tell you it's okay to give up on your dreams, it's usually because they either don't believe in your potential or have none in themselves.

A woman alone is an unstoppable force, but women united can make history.

Just as a flower needs the sun, our souls need to hear messages of hope.

Nothing will change until you realize that you are not a victim but the victor in your story.

Teach your children kindness, and they will change the world.

Be yourself always.

Don't try to be the person next door, the person on the TV, or anyone else you admire.

Just be happy with who you are.

When you dare to accept yourself, you will become the person you are meant to be.

Let love fill your heart and hold onto it with all you have.

I want to spread kindness throughout the hearts of the world until my last day.

On that day, when my journey is complete, I hope to reach my destination, knowing that my mission was achieved.

You have a beautiful life right where you are.

When you are comfortable with rejection and failure, success is inevitable.

Our egos sometimes try hard to win over those who don't care about us.

Leave your ego behind and pursue meaningful relationships that fulfill your heart's desire.

Everything you see and hear influences the way you think about life.

Follow people with great minds, humble attitudes, and who are committed to improving the world.

Be organic, be authentic, and always choose to live honestly.

Pretending to be someone else will only crush your spirit and eat away at you from within.

What you truly seek is not something that exists outside of yourself.

Come back to your roots and discover all that is within you.

There is no better listener than God.

Talk to Him.

When the world is shattered, kindness is the only path leading to a brighter future.

We may doubt our place in this world sometimes but remember it is temporary, and your spirit will live on forever.

I would climb the highest mountain, swim to the depths of the deepest sea, and run through heaven to find my mighty Lord and tell Him how much we need His great love.

Don't let the vision of a perfect outcome get in the way of completing your goals and moving on to your next great achievement.

We are born with an immediate need to be held and comforted; this is who we are.

It's also in our nature to return what is given, and one of the best ways to feel love is by sharing it with others.

Throw yourself into the world without fear and expectations, and you'll find love.

The person who lays down their sword and gives up on the war within themselves will see the promise of a new day and the world that can be.

You can find happiness by breaking down the walls you created to protect yourself and accept people as they are.

Stop fearing the worst in others and expect the best.

Time does not care what we have scheduled and will not wait for our convenience.

However, cherished memories can be a sanctuary where time is not invited.

Kindness changes everything for the better.

Your appreciation will change many lives and offer hope to those struggling to find it.

I would rather run through the hottest of flames chasing after my dreams than seek the shade and dream of my potential.

A world with no heart is of no value to anyone.

Don't be a dreamer who only envisions the result but forgets the struggle to get there.

Let your kindness be like a flower, open and waiting for the sun to shine on a new day.

Standing firm in front of your enemies shows your power, but when you forgive, it shows your inner strength.

I have the utmost respect for people who've endured hardships but still choose to live a life of kindness and forgiveness.

In the realm of the mind, where peace exists, there is no room for terror.

When you believe in
your goals, the
chains that keep you
from pursuing your
dreams will break
away, and you will
be free.

Forgiveness is about destroying the anger within and returning to love.

Love is the most
beautiful feeling
that dares to be
shared by those
who give all.

I sometimes imagine a different life.

Nevertheless, my heart draws me back to what I can do today.

The greatest tragedy is that we ought to live a beautiful life, yet so many of us are hurting and desperate to be loved.

When you humble
yourself to God and
understand His
majesty, you will
receive His peace.

Hard work wins the race, but kindness brings the crowd to their feet.

Experience helps you understand life, and understanding life will lead to wisdom.

The best remedy for an unkind heart is a kind act.

Narcissists will scheme and make plans to benefit themselves over the greater good.

Be careful when they tickle your ears with compliments because a knife in the back may not be far behind.

We control how we perceive our experiences and, as a result, how we respond in life.

So many of us respond emotionally without considering perspectives and, unfortunately, miss out on real growth.

The difference between feeling at home and feeling alone is the company you keep.

It's easy to be positive with kind people, but when the worst of us test your patience, stay strong and show them your example.

You've fought, healed, and grown as no one else could.

Now it's your turn to shine and share your light with the world.

True change is rarely accomplished alone, but support from a loved one can move mountains and change lives.

Hate does not have enough power to defeat love, but love has enough power to conquer the world.

Being kind is the greatest evidence of faith.

Normalize making peace with your mistakes.

Don't let it hold you back or ruin your confidence.

Learn from it and move forward.

I hope your smile brings warmth to a million souls.

I long to see you dance in this life to a song that never ends.

May your happiness never fade and last forevermore.

Although we cannot stop time, we can breathe in a moment and spend eternity in a thought.

It is God who gives you a gentle heart and beautiful people to love.

Choosing God instead of the world can be one of the hardest choices you make, but you will never regret it.

21695302R00115